We're from Indonesia

Emma Lynch

www.heinemann.co.uk/library
Visit our website to find out more information about **Heinemann Library** books.

To order:
☎ Phone 44 (0) 1865 888066
▤ Send a fax to 44 (0) 1865 314091
▢ Visit the Heinemann Bookshop at www.heinemann.co.uk/library to browse our catalogue and order online.

First published in Great Britain by Heinemann Library, Halley Court, Jordan Hill, Oxford OX2 8EJ, part of Harcourt Education.
Heinemann is a registered trademark of Harcourt Education Ltd.

Editorial: Jilly Attwood and Kate Bellamy
Design: Ron Kamen and Celia Jones
Illustrations: Darren Lingard
Photographer: Beth Evans
Picture Research: Maria Joannou and Erica Newbery
Production: Séverine Ribierre

Originated by Ambassador Litho Ltd
Printed and bound in China by South China Printing Company

ISBN 0 431 11947 3
09 08 07 06 05
10 9 8 7 6 5 4 3 2 1

British Library Cataloguing in Publication Data

Lynch, Emma
  We're From Indonesia
  959.8'04

A full catalogue record for this book is available from the British Library.

Acknowledgements

The publishers would like to thank the following for permission to reproduce photographs:

Harcourt Education pp. **30a, 30c**; Harcourt Education pp. **5a, 5b, 5c, 6, 7a, 7b, 8a, 8b, 9, 10a, 10b, 11, 12a, 12b, 13a, 13b, 14, 15a, 15b, 16a, 16b, 17a, 17b, 18a, 18b, 19a, 19b, 20a, 20b, 21a, 21b, 22, 23a, 23b, 24a, 24b, 25a, 25b, 26a, 26b, 27a, 27b, 28a, 28b, 29a, 29b, 30b** (Beth Evans).

Cover photograph of school children from Indonesia, reproduced with permission of Harcourt Education/ Beth Evans.

Many thanks to Adlina, Dihan, Noppy and their families.

Our thanks to Diyan Leake for her assistance in the preparation of this book.

Every effort has been made to contact copyright holders of any material reproduced in this book. Any omissions will be rectified in subsequent printings if notice is given to the publishers.

The paper used to print this book comes from sustainable resources.

Contents

Words appearing in the text in bold, **like this**, are explained in the Glossary.

 Find out more about Indonesia at
www.heinemannexplore.co.uk

Where is Indonesia?

To learn about Indonesia we meet three children who live there. Indonesia is a country in Asia. It is made up of lots of islands.

▲ This is a map of Indonesia. The capital city of Indonesia is Jakarta.

There are many small islands in Indonesia. Some of the larger islands have mountains and **volcanoes**. The weather in Indonesia is **tropical**.

Meet Adlina

Adlina is seven years old. She comes from a small village near Jakarta on the island of Java. She lives with her mother, father and sister.

◀ Adlina and her family are Muslims.

6

Adlina helps her parents around the house. She washes up the dishes. She also cleans her bedroom and helps in the garden.

Adlina's father

◄ Adlina's family live in a house made of bricks and **bamboo**.

Adlina's mother

Adlina

Adlina's sister

7

Adlina's school

Adlina goes to school five mornings a week. School starts at seven in the morning. Adlina walks to school with her best friend Kaina.

◀ Kaina lives next door to Adlina.

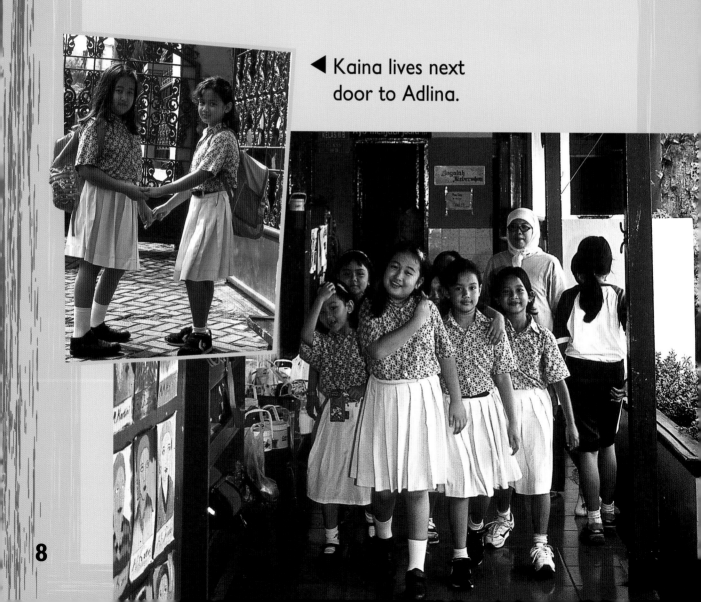

▲ This is Adlina's class.

Adlina enjoys school. She hopes to go to university one day. She learns Indonesian language and history, maths, religion, science, English and art.

Playing

Adlina does not have any homework. After school she likes to play with her friends. She plays *dampu* with Kaina. *Dampu* is a bit like hopscotch.

▼ Adlina has lots of friends at school to play with too.

All the boys and girls at Adlina's school play football. After school they all play football together in the playground.

▲ Their coach talks to them before they go out to play football.

Work in Indonesia

Many people in Indonesia work by making or growing things. Most of the work is done by people, not machines. People make bricks by hand, for example.

▼ Sand is gathered from the sea and rivers to make **cement**.

People also grow food, such as rice, to eat or to sell. What is made or grown can be sold to people in Indonesia or to other countries.

◀ Coconuts are picked for their fruit and their oil.

▼ Rice needs water and heat to grow well.

Meet Dihan

Dihan is seven years old. He lives in a town called Yogyakarta, on the island of Java. Dihan lives in a house with his mother, father, grandmother and four uncles.

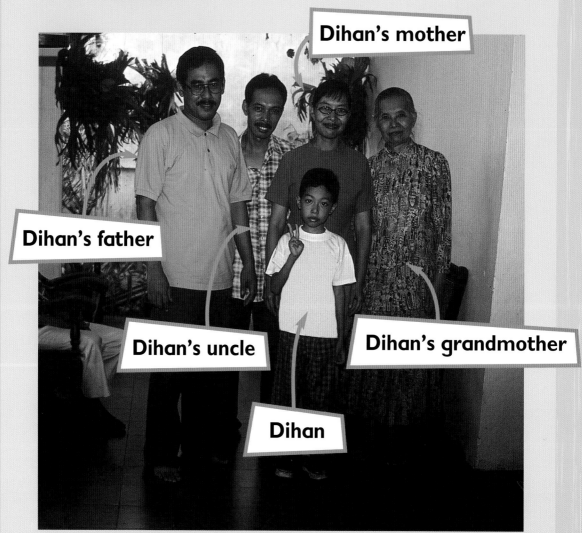

Dihan's mother

Dihan's father

Dihan's uncle

Dihan's grandmother

Dihan

▼ Dihan likes to pretend he is a Tyrannosaurus rex when he is eating!

Dihan's mother cooks. Everyone shares big plates of food. They use their fingers to eat. Dihan's favourite food is noodles.

At school

Dihan goes to school six mornings a week. He enjoys school and does well in his lessons. Dihan's parents buy him new books when he does really well at school.

◄ Dihan lives near to his school, so he walks there.

Dihan uses an ▶
abacus to help
him with maths.

Dihan has lessons in science, religion,
maths and art. He also learns
Indonesian and Javanese language
and history.

Dihan's afternoons

After school, Dihan helps at home. He cleans his room, the backyard, and the garden. Dihan likes to play outside or read with his friends.

◀ Dihan and his friends love playing football.

18

Dihan's father owns a workshop that prints T-shirts. Dihan has a job too. He makes **origami** animals for his uncle to print in a newspaper.

Dihan gets paid ▶ for designing origami animals!

▼ Dihan likes watching his father work.

Tourism

Many **tourists** visit Indonesia. Lots of people like to go to the island of Bali. It has **volcanoes**, sandy beaches and **tropical** forests.

volcano

The Indian Ocean ▶ around Bali is warm.

Tourists enjoy walking up the volcanoes. They can also do water sports on the sea. Tourists like to visit the old temple **ruins** of Borobudur.

▼ The Borobudur temple is on the island of Java.

Meet Noppy

Noppy is eight years old. She lives in a small village in Bali, near the sea. Noppy lives with her parents, sister, grandparents, aunt and uncles.

Noppy's house ▶ is made of **bamboo**, stone, wood and brick.

Noppy's mother

Noppy's sister

Noppy's father

Noppy

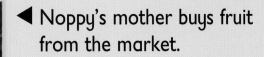
◀ Noppy's mother buys fruit from the market.

▼ Noppy likes eating fried rice with egg and chicken.

Noppy's family get water from a **well** outside the house. They grow their own vegetables, and keep pigs and chickens. The family sit on the floor to eat.

23

Noppy at school

Noppy goes to school six mornings a week. At school they learn Indonesian and Balinese language, maths, **martial arts**, science, art, dancing, music, religious studies and flower arranging.

◀ Noppy's class help at school by brushing the yard.

Noppy likes playing with her friend Sintya. They like singing and dancing and playing hide-and-seek. At school they play jumping games.

Noppy's life

Noppy's family and friends are **Hindus**. They pray three times a day at home or in a temple. Noppy wears a **traditional** Hindu dress when she prays. It is called a *kabaya*.

Noppy's family have ▶ a **shrine** at home.

◀ Noppy prays by their family's shrine.

▲ Noppy and her sister like to chase the hens around their yard!

Sometimes Noppy and her family visit the beach. Noppy likes to swim in the warm sea! Her family also go to visit other relatives for a meal.

Crafts

Indonesia is famous for its patterned cloth. It is called **batik**. Many women work in batik workshops. They draw pictures and patterns on cloth.

▲ A special wax pen is used to draw on the cloth.

Some beautiful pottery is made in Indonesia too. The pottery is made from red clay. People buy pots to decorate their homes and gardens.

Many people work in ▶ pottery workshops.

Indonesian fact file

Flag **Capital city** **Money**

Jakarta

Rupiah

Religion
• Most people in Indonesia are **Muslims**. There are some **Hindus** and Christians too.

Language
• Bahasa Indonesia is the official language of Indonesia. English and other Indonesian languages are also spoken.

Try speaking Bahasa Indonesia!
Selamat pagi .... Good morning.
Apa kabar? .... how are you?
Terima kasih .... Thank you.

 Find out more about Indonesia at
www.heinemannexplore.co.uk

Glossary

abacus frame with rods that beads are move along to do sums in maths

bamboo hard, hollow stem of a giant grass that can be used for building

batik cloth decorated with designs drawn with wax

cement paste that hardens and is used to stick bricks or stones together

Hindu a follower of the Hindu religion

martial arts fighting sport that has become an art

Muslim someone whose religion is Islam

origami special way of folding paper to make animal and flower shapes

ruins what is left of a building after it has fallen down

shrine special place or object that people pray in front of

tourist someone who is visiting on holiday

traditional something that has been going for a very long time without changing

tropical hot and muggy, with lots of rain

volcano mountain that has a hole down into the Earth. Sometimes melted rock and ash erupt from it.

well hole in the ground where people can get water

More books to read

Around the World: Food, Margaret Hall (Heinemann Library, 2002)

Continents: Asia, Leila Foster (Heinemann Library, 2002)

Letters from Around the World: Indonesia, David Cumming (Zero to Ten, 2004)

Index

Titles in the *We're from...* series include:

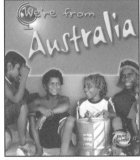

Hardback   0 431 11935 X

Hardback   0 431 11951 1

Hardback   0 431 11946 5

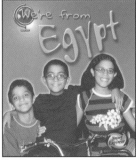

Hardback   0 431 11932 5

Hardback   0 431 11937 6

Hardback   0 431 11933 3

Hardback   0 431 11947 3

Hardback   0 431 11949 X

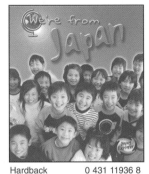

Hardback   0 431 11936 8

Hardback   0 431 11948 1

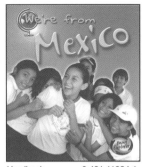

Hardback   0 431 11934 1

Hardback   0 431 11950 3

Find out about the other titles in this series on our website www.heinemann.co.uk/library